PREFACE

*

For many years, the energy to expand education for our children and protecting them from the evil that exists on this planet has diminished and it has been set aside due to politics.

Our politicians seem to forget that the only reason they are where they are today as successful Presidents, Senators, Representatives, Congressman, Governors, Mayors etc.; is because of the term *EDUCATION!!*

I fail to grasp the concept of why education is never the number one issue in our country – "America." That in and of itself is deserving of the utmost scrutiny.

Every nominee for Presidency should make providing significant education, protection, and safety for "ALL" of our children their number one agenda.

Indeed, the future belongs to our children. The next President, Senator etc.; will be one of our children.

Furthermore, the many ways our world functions, operates and remains consistent in providing a meaningful way of surviving will unequivocally depend on how our children are educated.

Without an education our society will remain in chaos, divided, and lack the elementary understanding of moral behavior, integrity and what it means to be a proven American.

If what I am saying is wrong, then why is it that racism continues to plague our country and our children must witness the countless violent encounters stemming from racism?

What is more, is that educating our children on their right to protest, the significance and history of protesting is in our age an essential conversation that is needed at an early age – why is this?

Why in the 21st Century where social media has provided a means to learn about and communicate with people who are of different races must we (the parents) tutor our children about segregation, white supremacy, racism, and why it continues?

Those who govern our country have misplaced the obvious need of an education and replaced the value, importance, and historical perception of an education with economics, politics and more economics and politics, but never education, education and more education.

Would it be wrong to say that economics has a direct link to education? Is education not the source of knowing how to control an economy?

Is it safe to purport that the economy must have a steady flow of job growth in order to prevent another great depression?

If so, then who keeps the economy from crashing? No doubt it is the employees who have GED's, High School Diplomas and College Degrees. Thus, without education there would be no economy!

I write this treatise to remind, if not educate those who may have forgotten or those who are interested in obtaining a profound understanding on the importance of education.

Within this treatise you will find brief but remarkably interesting topics related to education, racism, politics, and the United States Constitution.

Education is not just a key or a copy of a key. Rather, education is that unique magical key with many ridges that can open the multiple doors that are waiting to be opened.

I have presented a distinctive way of explaining what education means by providing a word and meaning for every letter in the term "*EDUCATION.*"

Each letter represents the ridges on that magical key with a concise elucidation connecting every letter together – essentially forming the word – *EDUCATION.*

My hope is that this treatise can motivate people in general to jump into the world of seeking useful

knowledge and experience the remarkable consequences of it.

I also hope that this treatise can ignite a serious conversation about the extreme need of a pervasive educational system that focuses on educating "ALL" Americans (especially children) on not just Math, Science, Social Studies,

Language Arts etc.; but also, about racism and how evil it is.

CHAPTER 1

EDUCATION

*

The word *"Education"* comes from the verb *"Educate,"* which means:

"To provide with schooling; to develop mentally and morally; also: to provide with information." (Webster's Dictionary)

Thus, education is the action or process of teaching, learning, and training the mind.

This act or process commences at an early age. it is for this very reason that schooling for children begins at the Pre-K and kindergarten level.

Schooling is first in preparing a child's mind for the reality of life which they are yet to conceive.

As they are learning subjects, topics, behavior, responsibilities, and history, they develop a mode or way of thought that builds principles and basic understanding regarding the difference between right and wrong.

In doing so a child's mind conforms to a standard of right and correct behavior.

An elementary mental and moral development helps children process information and accept knowledge with the ability to distinguish facts from falsehood, while maintaining their innocence.

Thus, if racism were to be a school subject the existence of such evil would be destroyed and morality in America would ascend.

There is no disputing the fact that it is only by way of education that racism would become the past and unity among races would become the future.

The inception stages of education are vital and beyond important – in fact, they are *CRUCIAL!!*

Throughout these stages a child's mind soaks up information like a sponge and whatever information is received becomes a part of their memory.

Therefore, all that they are taught and their intellect trains to remember is without a doubt what determines their thoughts and actions as they develop mentally.

The point being made, is that there is an inseparable nexus between *education* and *morale*. Therefore, in the event that education is lacking, so will morality.

When the process of mental evolvement is interrupted due to the mind being deprived of a fundamental education, the results will continue to be what we are witnessing today and have been observing for decades – racism, criminal behavior, a pervasive

spread of homeless people, public assistance, division, and the list goes on.

Education/Knowledge is a necessity not a privilege. Whenever anyone becomes complacent with having basic knowledge – just enough to get by, then they have by nature forsaken the path to true success in substitution for nescience.

Education is like a brick building. Without a foundation won't a building fall apart?

Similarly, the absence of an education, causes human morality, excellence, integrity, and intellect to diminish and dissipate until one comes to be mindless and eventually benighted.

Sleep time is over America! It is time to wake up and make obtaining an education the primary concern in this country, and in everyone's life.

CHAPTER 2

DETERMINES

*

The word *"Determines"* comes from the verb *"Determine,"* which means:

"To fix conclusively or authoritatively; to come to a decision; settle; resolve; to fix the form or character of beforehand; ordain; regulate; to find out limits; to bring about as a result." (Webster's Dictionary)

The conclusive and or authoritative decision to become a lawyer, a doctor, a businessperson, or whatever one desires to be in life comes from a thought that originated by way of education.

It is an education that determines a person's form of character and fortunate or unfortunate lifestyle result.

The second a person assumes to feel appeased and complete with respect to an education, that person will consequently limit their potential and settle for what was wrongfully concluded to be a prosperous outcome.

For instance: Universities and Colleges provide many different sets of degrees. However, we for some strange reason limit the possibility of advancing in a particular area of expertise simply because what we may earn weekly is in our mind enough to pay the monthly routine bills.

This way of thinking is typical and unfortunate. I say this because at any given moment responsibilities can multiply.

Furthermore, relationships occur, children are conceived and just that fast the list of expenditures expand exponentially.

The advantages of a continuous process to educating oneself for hopes of attaining a Higher Degree are most certainly superior.

Not one person in America should accept ignorance as a

permanent position while having the ability to learn, comprehend and apply knowledge generally or specifically knowing that education determines their outcome.

Here, we discern how detrimental education is in determining a person's limits, character, and end-result.

CHAPTER 3

UNCONDITIONALLY

*

The word *"Unconditionally"* comes from the verb *"condition,"* which means:

"To put into proper condition for action or use; to adapt; modify; or mold to respond in a particular way; to modify so that an act or response previously associated with one stimulus becomes associated with another." (Webster's Dictionary)

I conjugate the word "unconditionally" with the word "education," because it is indispensable to point out the fact that education is not and cannot be limited in any sort of way.

For instance: The pre-requisite to developing a successful career, ascending to the top, being triumphant in your future goals, expanding your intellectual capacity, establishing unswerving integrity, exploring substantial opportunities, and sustaining a fathomless degree of nobility all depends on the level of education you obtain.

Thus, outcomes are predicated upon education and nothing of the inverse is possible.

Look at this analogy; education is like the ocean. Both are immense and provide guidance. Traveling through the vast ocean patiently waiting to disembark at a predetermined destination is analogous to an excursion through the highways of education and persevering without interdiction to procure the knowledge needed to secure a meaningful life and arrive at a desired terminus by choice due to being relentless and remaining steadfast.

To fully understand that education has no ambit, one must look at all forms of education. Indeed, education is not restrictive to subjects or information learned throughout every school year including college.

Clearly, talent would be a senseless gift absent the educational process that explicates the purpose of a thing which a special artistic aptitude relates to.

In other words, there is a clear distinction between a talented basketball player and the basketball itself.

Not every basketball player can shoot accurately in a consistent manner.

It is the natural endowment of a person that allows them to develop a precise method of shooting the ball and making it in the hoop.

However, this cannot occur without first being educated on the purpose of a basketball.

Talent does not inform us of the rationale behind the creativity of a basketball and how it is used to shoot from short and or long distance, bounced on the floor, bounced between our legs and passed around.

Once again, the need for education as demonstrated here is inevitable and essential.

Outside of being educated, people would not know anything about everything that exists today.

The reality is dogmatic; education has no boundaries, no stoppage and is unconditionally the rationalization behind prosperity, while ignorance is the father of deficiency.

CHAPTER 4

CAREERS

*

The word *"Career"* is a noun, which means:

"An occupation or profession followed as a life's work. (Webster's Dictionary)

Careers are subservient on the quality of education derived.

Thus, the more knowledge accepted into a person's memory bank – particularly on a specific subject, the more advanced a person will be.

So, if someone is studying to become a medical doctor, it would be incumbent upon that person to prepare and anticipate a jaded journey that entails years of learning to be considered a proficient medical doctor.

The amount of studying a person invests inserts them in what I consider an educational category that's relative to the career level that person perfects.

This educational category consists of three levels:

"Low Class," "Middle Class," and "High Class."

Careers ultimately fall into one of these three categories placing emphasis on the level of education one acquires.

The three levels mentioned are the equivalence of an "Associates Degree," "Bachelor's Degree," and "Master's Degree."

Each level of degree a person earns will raise their status, which will define their career.

Considering the aforementioned, I strongly encourage people in general to never settle for a "Low Class" education. Settling for a "Low Class" education may designate you by your own fault, within the stages of ignorance.

Although the term *ignorance* may sound harsh, the reality is that a person's actions not to pursue an education is by definition an ignorant choice. Indeed, the term ignorance is the total opposite of the term knowledge? Therefore, the term ignorance as it relates to not seeking an education, only represents the poor choice of not wanting to pursue an education.

Having an ignorant state of mind can hinder a person's progress if they had plans to reach the "High Level" which translates to a career of "High Rank" and "Status."

Careers, which are like professions that are not inherited are the parity of an education being a necessity that must be pursued in a persistent fashion.

We all have volition. We can either explore the fundamental and deep fields of knowledge which will ensure our place in the future, or we can let time and opportunities pass us by.

Careers are built from the ground up. Each course/class a person takes resulting in an amount of knowledge accepted, is one brick added to that person's substructure.

But ignorance on the other hand can be dangerous and have the devastating impact of a strong wind, and even a tornado depending on how long a person allows themselves to habituate within the sphere of ignorance.

A strong wind may knock off some bricks, but the groundwork will likely remain stable. However, unlike a strong wind, a tornado can easily destroy the entire substructure.

A "strong wind" here is analogous to *"slight ignorance,"* and a "tornado" is more like the consequences of falling into a category I refer to as *"stagnated ignorance."*

The difference between the two is that *"slight ignorance"* is the temporary abdication of educational studies – nevertheless, if continued can inadvertently slip into the preliminary stages of *"stagnated ignorance,"* which is much more difficult to rebound from.

If anyone was to find that they are suffering from *"slight ignorance"* or *"stagnated ignorance,"* the following questions need to be asked:

1) How important is it to start, have and maintain a career?

2) Is remaining at a "Low Class" sufficient enough to sustain a desired and successful lifestyle?

3) Are the ramifications surrounding a "Low Class" gratification understood?

The effects of abandoning knowledge and being satisfied with a "Low Class" education can present futuristic problems involving a low income and an accumulation of bills which cannot be satisfied while only earning minimum wage pay and having no other assistance.

Furthermore, an individual may aspire a certain position within their place of employment, and when it is time for that individual to be interviewed for that position, they may be asked the following questions:

1) What do you know about the position you have applied for?

2) If hired for that position, how would you deal with X, Y and Z?

The general reply would be based on the knowledge

that person has acquired in that particular area.

Unfortunately, the amount of knowledge and experience acquired may mean nothing or little next to nothing.

This brings us back to the "effects" of abandoning knowledge?

Realistically speaking, what parent wouldn't want for their child to accomplish their goals in life and establish a career which as a direct result of an education comes with a life of peace, security and happiness?

None of the above mentioned is possible however, without an education.

Parents must play a part in their children's future by stressing to them the gravity and importance of knowledge and its reverse meaning.

Additionally, parents must also recognize that an example is always best understood and followed by a child when their parents are the primary actors.

CHAPTER 5

ASCENSION

*

The word *"Ascension"* comes from the verb *"Ascend"* which means:

"To move upward; mount; climb; to succeed; to occupy." (Webster's Dictionary)

Possessing qualitative characteristics and having the ability, motivation and desire to pursue a career that's most attractive and pleasing, provides a favorable indication that being successful is evident, and the probability of moving upward in a position within a major company or in any form of business in general is highly likely.

One must have a compelling and unbounded thirst for knowledge if dreams are to become realities.

If the thirst or hunger for knowledge isn't sincere, then the reality of the dream to execute a high rank or status in life is no more than a fantasy and the experience of an unpropitious chimerical event.

In all actuality, knowledge is the sister of education,

which helps design and fashion the many ridges found on that magical key.

While knowledge helps shape and sharpen the ridges on that magical key, it is the beauty of a well-developed education that allows the ridges to open the quantum doors of opportunities.

Moreover, it is of great importance to know and understand that knowledge is of two types:

1) Knowledge of information.

2) Knowledge of understanding.

"Knowledge of information" is when the brain receives general informative data and other additional information that may be pertinent, essential, fundamental and or thorough going.

Nevertheless, a person does not entirely comprehend the import of the information received, consequently losing out on the opportunity to enjoy the expressive lore that may be detrimental to futurity decision making.

What is meant by the statement, *"does not entirely comprehend"* has absolutely nothing to do with being able to read, learn and listen, or lacking aptitude. Rather, it has everything to do with a person's actions.

Without assertive implementation of information that may be relative to a dire situation with enormous influential consequences, the knowledge obtained is futile.

This is what is meant by the said statement, *"does not entirely comprehend."*

"Knowledge of understanding" is quite the opposite. When a person understands whatever intake of knowledge/information they have received and accepted, such understanding will be observed through their behavior.

Put differently, a person's behavior/actions will reflect their comprehension of the knowledge accepted, not just obtained.

The divarication between *"obtaining knowledge"* and *"accepting knowledge"* is substantial. Obtaining knowledge/information is artless. Lore is gained but the application of it may not be imperative.

Accepting knowledge/information on the other hand, is the self-encouraging willingness capitulated in exchange for cerebral guidance which features ascension.

Furthermore, to ascend intellectually or in berth and in life universally, accumulating factors must exist.

Insight, good sense, a wise attitude, fair judgement, profundity and the sage are distinctive elements necessary to soar and advance to a higher status across the spectrum.

The mentioned attributes display wisdom and dictates resolutions, conclusions, decisiveness and unwavering toughness in action and in the power of free will.

Having wisdom demonstrates awareness, cognizance and perception which is the nexus to mental capabilities evincing competency and naturally acquired skills – indeed, proficient skills.

When vetted for a higher position involving empowerment, the psychological description presented above is climacteric.

Thus, a person without wisdom is a person without understanding, which is an unfortunate person who failed to inhale the magnificent scent of education.

The inestimable value of education is sadly enervated and has been designated to third place behind politics and economics because most of our politicians are careless and people in general are uninterested in the true value of education, which is unequivocally a fascinating process with endless options leading to amazing achievements.

CHAPTER 6

TRIUMPHANT

*

The word *"Triumphant"* comes from the verb *"Triumph,"* which means:

To obtain victory; to prevail; to celebrate victory or success exultantly."

The relation between education and triumphant is a direct one.

The level of education delimitates the extent of exultation. But the choice is yours.

Circumscription on educating yourself will inhibit

and reduce the degree in celebrating a victorious career of self-employment and universal employment at a high rank and being didactic by way of comporting.

The antithesis of victory is losing, failing and being unfortunate.

Thus, triumphant can be considered an act that cannot be followed through without the pre-requisite of education.

For example: If a future war was anticipated between America and an adverse country; in order to win, America's representatives – such as Generals, Admirals, and their like must have an in depth understanding of how the enemy may attack, what type of weaponry they may have access to, and the number of damages that can be expected with respect to casualties.

Unsuccessful outcomes are eminent when the requisites of learning, teaching, and all aspects of education are disregarded as unnecessary.

It is far too often in retrospect that regret of not seeking proper educational knowledge /information is felt.

However, remorse is only half the battle. And, for some, it may be too late to establish a strong appetence for the love and sincere desire of beneficial knowledge.

Failing or falling short in certain areas (like losing in a meaningless baseball game) is disparate from failing in a potential life changing examination, or from falling short in making progressive and decisive decisions that in turn may affect a person's life forever, simply because educating themselves was deserted, forsaken and left alone to the point of no return.

Complete abandonment of consistent educational development is an arrest of the mind, personal autonomy and a person's ability along with their potential, placing that person in a bubble with those who have accepted failure and defeat – rather than triumph.

In between the act of winning and losing, lies cheating – a form of a "corrupt victory," but actually means losing.

Cheating demoralizes the person who is doing the cheating, and rightfully places them in the category of those who are perceived as being defrauders, swindlers, tricksters and cozeners.

More importantly, words like integrity, honor, soundness, completeness and character do not subsist in the mind of a person who likes to cheat.

In short, laziness and slothfulness and coalesced

with acquisitiveness, avidity and greed best describes the mindset of a cheater.

The terms *"triumphant"* and *"cheating"* have absolutely no relation. Indeed, cheating is the exclusive enemy of triumph.

The negative connection between triumph and cheating leads me to state the obvious:

It is undoubtedly a fact, that a lack of education by choice haplessly adduces circumstances where a person seemingly desists their moral integrity for a short cut that has no value, and the efficacy is contaminative and corruptive.

Pure victory erects reputation, shadowed with homage, obeisance, prestige, praise and respect.

Hence, in order to be victorious in life, an education must obviously exist in its entirety and shadowed by honorable behavior.

CHAPTER 7

INTELLECT

&

INTEGRITY

*

The word *"Intellect"* is a noun which means:

"The power of knowing; the capacity for knowledge; the capacity for rationale or intelligent thought esp. when highly developed; a person with great intellectual powers." (Webster's Dictionary)

The word *"integrity"* is a noun which means:

"Adherence to a code of values; incorruptibility; soundness; completeness." (Webster's Dictionary)

Animals are incongruously different from humans. They do not possess the power of intellect which for humans is used to rationalize thoughts and make considerable decisions with sound purpose.

The power of intellect places accent on the blatant need for educational erudition. As the cerebral admits lore, the intellect cultivates and strengthens greatly.

Children are a perfect example of this fact. For instance:

Every day when children go to school, they return home with a new word, a new sentence and how that word functions in a sentence.

Each stage mirrors intellectual improvement. The maxim that *"the mind is a terrible thing to waste"* is veridical.

Thus, excellent innate qualities succors with producing splendid results while an emaciated apperception originates very negative and at times frightful outcomes.

Accordingly, educating the mind with propitious wisdom

is a preventive mechanism for creating appalling consequences.

Furthermore, benignant information not only obviates intolerable endings, it also agnates undeviatingly to the concept of integrity.

Put differently, education is the derivation and antecedent of completeness.

Henceforth, a person with dignified intellect adheres to a code of values and cannot be debased.

That which links intellect and integrity is incontestably education.

Clearly, it is education that exploits the intellect which in turn allows the mind to fully foresee and arrange a rationalized process of logical thinking – rather than an irrationalized process of impulsive reactions.

Applying logical thinking, rules, principles and intellectual attentiveness in everyday events, occurrences and or incidents entails having a profound structure of balance and thoughtfulness which is essentially educed and extracted from an educational training of the mind.

Furthermore, education has an interrelationship with mental acuteness, sophistication, intellect and integrity thereby making education the number one artistical adventure every human being with a sound mind should embark on.

Diametrical to this view supports the irrational thoughtlessness that many suffer from when making poor choices that only frame and fabricate a counter fancy that *"the mind is not a terrible thing to waste."*

Moreover, superciliousness, pridefulness and overly convinced of one's superiority and self-import is one of many reasons for an educational failure.

To put it straightforward, arrogance is diabolical; therefore, it is the archenemy of education, knowledge, ascension, triumphant, intellect/integrity, opportunity and nobility.

When the cerebral experiences the poison of haughtiness and insolence, destruction is evident.

With that said, arrogance is a disease that has a cure, and of course, that cure is an education.

Thus, suffering from arrogance can be rectified, but abetment is needed, and the resuscitation process of an education must take place immediately.

However, while assistance is available, the doctor (*Education*) can only proscribe the medication (*Knowledge*) to a patient who's willing to accept and benefit from the cure.

Ignoring the truth is a form of resistance and indicative of the free will to remain in a state of arrogance and denial.

Assistance is always available for anyone who is ready to accept and benefit from the cure.

Nevertheless, it is upon the proprietor of pridefulness to reverse course and inject pure and correct knowledge into their brain thereafter producing *sound intellect* – thoughtfulness and completeness which when combined, defines *integrity*.

CHAPTER 8

OPPORTUNITY

*

The word *"Opportunity"* is a noun which means:

"A favorable combination of circumstances; time and place; a chance for advancement." (Webster's Dictionary)

Opportunities are like doors; most open and close with keys, but there's only one key that can open quantum doors of opportunities and that magical key is *education*.

Further, the advantages of having an education are countless. To name a couple, let's commence with employment.

Certainly, resumes influence job interviews and a college degree identifies the areas where a college student specializes in which helps the interviewer make a predetermined decision prior to conducting the interview.

The more educational degrees or higher level of a specific college degree can only help heighten the chances of securing employment and landing an established position of major importance.

Those lacking college degrees, high school diplomas and GED's may find themselves job searching more often than others.

A person not in possession of a college degree, high school diploma or GED can be replaced at any given moment for someone who has the qualifications required.

While it is true that degrees from well-established Universities like Harvard University, Princeton University and or Yale University present a favorable advantage in procuring certain types of employment, community colleges and other Universities provide educational courses as well, which have aided in producing some of the most prevalent scholars, judges, lawyers, doctors etc., of our time.

Another advantage of having an education is the honorable perception perceived by others without the need to be physically present to witness the reality of someone's achievements.

Words like remarkable, fascinating, brilliant, genius and or intelligent are commonly used to describe a person who has not only attained a high level of education but has also implemented the knowledge acquired in areas of great significance.

A door will only open when the correct key is used. Likewise, opportunities become acquirable and attainable when the proper and correct education is being observed.

Each grade passed in school beginning at Pre-K up to 12th grade is the parity of the click sound made when a key is opening a closed door.

Every click sound represents confidence, safety, and guarantees that the future will be secure, stable, and perdurable.

Each click sound is also perpetual and does not end until the educative satisfactory goals are mastered.

Moreover, an Associate Degree, Bachelor's Degree, Master's Degree and PHD were invented for a reason.

Therefore, why stop and give up on education after obtaining an associate degree when at the top of the ladder is a PHD?

No doubt a lesser degree – like an associate degree will most definitely be sufficient to work in a major company, but a PHD would permit a person to create and establish their own lucrative business.

Thus, the opportunities and advantages with respect to having an education are crystal clear.

Furthermore, there are levels of status and rank for each one *(opportunities and advantages)* respectively.

However, the levels for both (opportunities and advantages) depend on the degree of education acquired, accepted, and implemented.

For every degree achieved, there will be a detailed and special opportunity/advantage, and the circumstances remarkably change as you upgrade and obtain a higher degree of education.

Hence, perennial education is the key for obtaining college degrees and it is the foundation which supports the unlimited number of opportunities and advantages that exist in America.

CHAPTER 9

NOBILITY

*

The word *"Nobility"* is a noun which means:

"The quality or state of being noble (well known, famous, notable, of high rank). (Webster's Dictionary)

The state of being noble can come from a birth right or from arduous work and dedication.

Devotion to years of educating oneself can be overwhelming, but the reward which awaits at the finish line is notable and worth the effort.

Therefore, having patience is mandatory. Surely, mastering patience (a common noun) and perseverance (a verb) are virtues that when practiced will permit the mind to persist and move forward during times of difficult studies.

Taking breaks are important, but I must stress the need to be incredibly careful not to unwittingly build a pattern of excess break periods which may lead to temporary abandonment of educational studies followed by permanent withdrawal.

Strong will, patience, forbearance, insistency, and a puissant desire are compulsory features every person should have when pursuing nobility.

Furthermore, the incipient steps of becoming famous or someone of high rank and status has everything to do with pedagogy.

At this juncture of this treatise, the intention behind concluding the last letter of the word *"EDUCATIO(N)"* with *"NOBILITY"* is pellucid.

Indeed, Careers, Ascension, Triumphant, Intellect/Integrity and opportunities encompass the laudable excellence of the term *"NOBILITY."*

However, within the fabrics of nobility rests education – the mother that nourishes and is amenable for the preferment's in each period associated for all the accomplishments crossing from one side of the equator to the other.

Nobility is the direct descendant of education which exhibits the benefits, significance, superiority, desirability, power, and consequences of anyone who fastens themselves upon a fascinating, entertaining and satisfying jaunt, but within the circumference of auspicious knowledge.

I close this chapter with the reminder that it is *"EDUCATION"* without a doubt that *DETERMINES,*

UNCONDITIONALLY, CAREERS, ASCENSION, TRIUMPHANT, INTELLECT/INTEGRITY, OPPORTUNITY, AND NOBILITY.

CHAPTER 10

RACISM

*

The word *"Racism"* is a noun which means:

"A belief that some races are by nature superior to others; also: discrimination based on such belief." (Webster's Dictionary)

Based on the definition, whoever has the above-mentioned belief will be considered a *"racist."*

Additionally, racial prejudice, racial bias and racial discrimination are all related terminologies connected to and no different from the term *"RACISM."*

Thus, a racist can be anyone with traits of prejudicial and discriminating beliefs.

Modifiers like – Anti Black, Anti White, Black Supremacist and White Supremacist were developed due to the historical enigmatic and mystifying intricate relationship involving two races with different skin complexions.

It would be remiss of me not to mention the fact that one race (White Americans) in the past did dominate and enslave another race - (Black Americans) for decades – a blatant reality that is well established in our history books.

Although, my general focus is to promote the need for schools to implement a subject specifically based on racism, its history and evil affects, I'm inclined to opine indicatively on the matter of contention surrounding the racially motivated division amongst Black and White Americans, which continues to torment our country – a disgrace chargeable to the exiguity of education acquired on the depth topic of *"RACISM."*

Based on my research, investigation, personal

experience, and ascertainment, I've concluded that racism is an overwhelming destructive psychosomatic illness combined with morbidity and pestilence.

The lack of assiduousness for decades by those who govern our country bewilders me.

It would be nonsensical to assume that Congress, the President of the United States, and all Representatives who represent America are oblivious with respect to the copious number of episodes and killings involving municipal white law enforcement officers and

Black Americans.

Those who are responsible for governing our country and keeping us safe can deliver an ultra-blow to racism by way of passing new meaningful legislation.

They have absolute power and authority to influence drastic changes.

Indeed, they write and pass the laws that are intended to govern society and establish public peace.

We need a Senate, a House of Representatives and a President who are educated on the efficacies of racism with the bona fide proclivity to find antidotes that can help reshape the noxious views that many Americans have on the hue of a person's skin.

Almost every disease in our planet has a cure; likewise, so does racism.

The prescription and healing agent is undoubtedly education.

If all our schools were to implement a comprehensive subject dealing with the topic of Racism in addition to Math, Science, Social Studies, Language Art, and other subjects taught, the future would seem promising.

Educating our children at a noticeably young age (starting at some point in elementary school) about the diabolical effects of racism would morally prepare them for the eventuality, and the events to come implicating onerous conversations and general encounters with people who have been misled and suffer from the poisonous apple *(RACISM)* given to them by friends and even family members who for many years have been misguided.

A profound educational subject on racism would bring awareness to our future generations providing them with illuminating radiation (pure knowledge on racism) that will burn the whispers of the Devil when he whispers prejudicial evilness into the hearts and thoughts of every American and human being in general.

Racism starts off like a virus in the air, and a person only becomes a racist when they are infected with the virus.

The obvious question is how does a person contract the virus *(Racism)*? The answer is uncompounded and simplistic; the deprivation of education on the inquiry of Racism has us confused and lost!

The lack of education is exactly why so many Americans have contracted the virus known as racism.

Wake up America! Must I continue to repeat that education is the key?

We must act against the insidious threats posed against our children and their future.

America is a great country, but ignorance and arrogance fan the flames of hate and racism, making our great country appear to be what it is today – one of the most racist countries on this planet.

My message to the protestors, teachers, principals, Congresspeople, law makers, all of America's Representatives, the current President of the United States and to those who genuinely care is to advocate for making *"Racism"* a primitive subject in all schools within America commencing at the elementary level and instructed in high schools and Universities/Colleges.

Rather than having mothers and fathers etc.; feeling the need to explain to their children (who will be the next generation in America) about racism, its history and the perverse actions of people who have been led astray (with respect to racism) why not have our schools implement public and private curriculums entailing racism?

Our educational system, which is properly equipped, can develop a methodical approach in schooling and training the mind of a child on the correct precept that racism is immoral, wicked, sinful, diabolical and malevolent thus, categorizing the thought of becoming a racist – dishonorable, ignoble, offensive and shameful.

Any thoughts diametric to this viewpoint will only support the irrational cognitive indolence that many suffer from.

This treatise is not intended to elaborate on the many details surrounding racism.

However, through this treatise my intentions is to provide the recipe, remedy and guidance to the key that can close the door on racial prejudice and open the door of love, happiness, and blindness to skin color etc.

I emphasize however, that the one and only key that subsists which can close the doors of racism and open the doors of love and unity in this great country of ours is *EDUCATION!*

CHAPTER 11

POLITICS

&

POLITICIANS

*

The word *"Politics"* is a noun which means:

"The art or science of government; of guiding or influencing governmental policy or winning and holding control over a government; political affairs or business; esp.; competition between groups or individuals for power and leadership." (Webster's Dictionary)

The word *"Politician"* is a noun which means:

"A person actively engaged in government or politics." (Webster's Dictionary)

I commence this chapter by stating the most obvious; *"Absolute Power Corrupts Absolutely."*

To proceed: Enjoying the Constitutional right to vote for a politician is half the battle when seeking change and better results in America.

The other half of the battle which is of the most importance is having an educational understanding on how a politician may operate when it comes to politics.

By definition, the typical politician engages in governmental politics and those politics include influencing governmental policy, winning sits in Congress, holding control over the government and competing against a rival party for power and leadership.

The art and science that comes with the territory of being a politician is quite unique.

Let me explain: Although, there are some honest politicians who are genuine or may appear to be sincere at first glance, (throughout the elect me process) the party, whether Republicans or Democrats who will become their colleagues expect loyalty of the upmost to their respective party, which essentially handcuffs and obstructs their original intent and promising agenda.

Furthermore, to get anything passed in Congress, a politician must give full support to a bill put together by the alligators (their party) that run the swamp.

This practice is called politics but resembles quid pro quo.

In any event, knowing the art and science of politics to some degree is desideratum.

In Congress, there are three types of groups of

politicians regardless of them being from the same party.

- The First Group: These are the newcomers, beginners, first-year students, learners, and neophytes.
- The Second Group: These are the sophomores, lower classmen and the under classmen.
- The Third Group: These are the seniors, elders, higher in rank and more advanced superiors.

Thus, with seniority comes precedence, priority, preferences, and status.

So, I ask a rhetorical question, which group of

politicians would anyone presume has the absolute power?

Politicians who run to obtain a seat in Congress for the first time are fully informed of the obstacles they will face once in office.

However, most of them still make false promises to their constituents or hopeful supporters in exchange for their votes.

The authentic political first-year student should not be naive. Rather than remain silent on the plight they will have to wrestle with if voted into office, they should be frank and honest by uttering statements such as "I will fight to make X, Y and Z happen," not "I promise if you vote for me, I will make certain that X, Y and Z will happen."

Being educated in the world of politics is not a necessity, but it is encouraging.

In fact, the right to vote would have a significant meaning and personal value dissimilar to a vote that simply joins another vote but is empty with no value, meaning or materialness.

Most Americans just vote for a party they have accepted for years.

We should be Americans who vote for politicians

whom we first investigated, studied and because of our due diligence we have learned those politicians' true values.

Unfortunately, there is no alternative system set up to help govern the United States of America.

We must rely on rotten and crooked politicians with hidden political agendas.

Nonetheless, the consequences of a person's vote can be substantial. Therefore, the fundamental educational understanding on how the art and science of politics functions is vital – indeed, its' imperative.

In my opinion, parties – such as Republicans and

Democrats are necessary for establishing the power and liberty of interpretation, different points of views and entitlement of having an opinion.

However, the corrupt principles, secrets and unethical behavior tolerated by both parties has brought America into a generation of complete divisiveness.

When compared to the generation of old, our modern-day Politicians are cowards, corrupt and worthless with no integrity.

Due to their reckless and careless behavior, the prestigious cognomen of our country – "United States of

America" has been replaced with the modern and more befitting title – "Divided States of America."

The so-called experts (not all of them) whom have been voted into office and have been placed in a position of dominance are entirely responsible for the unacceptable conduct that has contaminated and demoralized millions of Americans.

Further, when a United States citizen proclaims with conviction that they are a registered Republican or Democrat, they are assuring either party that their Guaranteed Constitutional

Right to vote belongs to them (Republicans/Democrats).

In other words, the freedom of owning an independent way of thinking becomes politicized when a United States citizen registers as a Republican or Democrat.

This argument becomes clear when we give attention to the terms "Blue" and "Red" states.

"Blue" states represent those U.S. citizens who have registered as Democratic voters and "Red" states represent those U.S. citizens who have registered as Republican voters.

Hence, when election season comes about, it is

expected that a U.S. citizen's right to vote will be their (Republicans/Democrats) privilege to claim the votes of millions of registered U.S. Citizens.

However, the beauty of registering as an independent voter even if your beliefs lean more to the right or left, is that you to get to control the outcome of the election process by independently choosing who you feel is the nominee most deserving of your vote.

Simply said, the right to vote is an independent right which should be exercised with a decent educational understanding on how the art and science of politics serve.

I can go on and on regarding our political system that involves dishonorable politicians, but again, my objective is to squarely emphasize on the extreme need and usefulness of an education and the general benefits concerning auspicious knowledge.

My hope is that this reminder benefits anyone interested in the extraordinary perception of education.

CHAPTER 12

UNITED STATES CONSTITUTION

*

The word *"Constitution"* is a noun which means:

"An established law or custom; the structure; composition or make up of something; the basic law in a politically or organized body; also: a document containing such law." (Webster's Dictionary)

In this chapter, which concerns the Constitution of

the United States of America,
I present four basic questions
for readers to cogitate over,
then answer this question: *"Is
the need to be educated on
the United States Constitution
of significant importance with
severe consequences?"*

1) Why was the *"Original"*
United States Constitution
and the *"Amended"*
Constitution (Bill of Rights)
created?

2) What is the difference
between the United States
Constitution as a whole and a
State Constitution?

3) Who is responsible for
interpreting the *"Original"*
United States Constitution
and the *"Amended"*
Constitution (Bill of Rights)?

4) What is the process for electing the President and Vice President of the United States of America?

If you do not know the answer to any of the fundamental questions presented above, then I implore you to take 15 minutes out of your day and start the process of educating yourself on the *"Original"* United States Constitution and the Bill of Rights – *"Amended"* Constitution.

Furthermore, unless a person is suffering from cretinism or a learning disability, being witless and ignorant of your fundamental "RIGHTS" is an issue that must be rectified at the first opportunity.

At any given moment anyone can experience an infringement upon one of their protected rights and may not even be cognizant of it.

In the reverse, someone may have lived through an encounter where they had mistakenly speculated that one of their rights were violated but were inexact.

The common people in general need not have the desire to want to become an attorney or a constitutional scholar in order to educate themselves in an attempt to familiarize themselves with the historical, and modern interpretation of the United States Constitution.

I cannot overly stress enough the import and need to have basic knowledge – particularly with respect to the First, Second, Fourth, Fifth, Sixth, Eight and Fourteenth Amendments of the United States Constitution. The mentioned Amendments are the most notable and distinguished Amendments that have been and continue to be the subject of the upmost scrutiny.

Moreover, an inspection and analysis of the said Amendments will never cease because these Amendments are mostly exercised, and or defiled on a symmetrical basis.

The indicated brings me to **_Question Number One_**:

"Why was the Original United States Constitution and the Bill of Rights created?"

Abridged Answer: The Original United States Constitution consisted of *"Eight Articles,"* chiefly dealing with how the three branches of government, (the House, Senate, and Office of the Presidency) and the United States Supreme Court would administer.

The implementation of the Eight Articles took place on September 17, 1787, during the Presidency of Go. Washington.

Thereafter, on March 4, 1789, the Original Constitution was "Amended" by Congress, and ratified in 1791.

The "Amendment" added ten more Articles known as the Bill Rights.

The main objective of the Bill of Rights, which is an element and augmentation of the Original United States Constitution was to protect and shield every American from all improper conduct involving the Federal Government.

Thus, the founding fathers were aware that the

government, if not restricted by placing boundaries on how far they could go would become oppressive ruffians abusing their power – simulating a tyrant.

Hence, the founding fathers created the Bill of Rights to protect all Americans/United States Citizens, not just the one percent (wealthy and rich Americans) from anticipated tyranny and abuse of authority by yours truly – the *"Federal Government."*

Question Number Two:

"What is the difference between the United States Constitution as a whole and a State Constitution?"

Abridged Answer: As explained above, the United States Constitution, particularly the Bill of Rights, was created to protect all Americans/Citizens from the improper conduct involving the Federal Government.

As for State Constitutions, (each State has their own Constitution) they were designed among other things to guard its residents from the improprieties involving State and or municipal law enforcement officers.

To be clear, both Constitutions are not identical and should not be misconstrued as such.

Furthermore, if any writings declared in any State

Constitution contradicts or opposes the United States Constitution, the latter overrides the former.

Question Number Three:

"Who is responsible for interpreting the Original Constitution and the Bill of Rights, and what's the difference between the two?"

Abridged Answer: This subject is of major importance, so please pay close attention.

Those responsible with deciphering and interpreting the United States Constitution are the Supreme Court Justices (9 Justices).

The Honorable Justices provide rules, principles, and

differences of opinions on highly controversial inquiries pertaining to the vague and ambiguous inscription of the Original United States Constitution and the Bill of Rights.

In short, there is so much more than what meets the eye when it comes to defining, interpreting, and comprehending the United States Constitution.

Thus, every word and sentence communicated in each Article of the United States Constitution is subject to a profound investigation, examination, exploration, and scrutiny by the Honorable Justices with the intention of elucidating the exact application.

As for the difference between the Original Constitution and the Bill of Rights, the Original Constitution mainly dealt with the description of authority that the House of Representatives, Senators, Presidents and the United States Supreme Court possessed.

With respect to the Bill of Rights, please refer to the *"Abridged Answer"* I gave to *"Question Number One."*

Question Number Four:

"What is the process for electing the President and Vice President of the United States of America?"

Abridged Answer: The said question may appear to have an obvious and simple answer, and many people will most likely say that the American people who vote elect the president and the President elects the Vice President.

However, the veracious response lies in Article Two (section 1) of the Original Constitution and in Article Twelve of the Amended Constitution.

The language in Article Twelve of the Amended Constitution is straightforward on how the President and Vice President are elected.

Article Twelve reads: "The ELECTORS shall meet in their respective states, and votes by ballot for President and Vice President (of the United States)."

Furthermore, Article Twelve goes on to read that after the *"ELECTORS"* transmit their votes to the President of the Senate, "the President of the Senate shall, in the presence of the Senate and House of Representatives, open all the certificates and votes shall then be counted; the person having the greatest number of votes for President, shall be the President."

Thus, the difference between the common people's vote and the elector's vote is that the common people *"choose"* whom they would *"like"* to be the President (not Vice President), and the elector's vote determines who *"will become"* the next President.

I am certain, that if anyone who had no notion prior to reading this treatise, that the process explicated in Article Twelve of the United States Constitution is how the President and Vice President of the United States are elected to Office, the information provided above would have sounded strange and outlandish.

Here, we imbibe the method on how the *"election"* process transpires.

As established in the United States Constitution, the American people *"choose"* but do not *"elect"* the President or Vice President of the United States of America.

In its stead, electors are appointed by Congress in every state to come together, provide their votes, and just like that the next President and Vice President are elected to represent the United States of America.

This process is referred to as the *"electoral process."*

Therefore, achieving millions of more votes than the other Presidential opponent, like Hillary Clinton accomplished over Donald

Trump in the 2016 election, unfortunately and sadly betokens nothing!

Earlier I intimated the First, Second, Fourth, Fifth, Sixth, Eight and Fourteenth Amendments of the United States Constitution as being the most notable, controversial, and distinguished Amendments.

The following should furnish a limpid perception with respect to the imprecision and obscurity of the language within the United States Constitution, which continues to be questionable and subject to controversy.

Let us briefly review the Seven Amendments I referred

to above, beginning with a portion of the First Amendment.

Amendment I*:* As established in Amendment I; "Congress shall make no law … abiding the freedom of speech … or the right of the people peaceably to assemble."

Does this mean that people are free to say whatever they wish? The answer is unequivocally NO!

For example: If anyone were to make public threats of harming the President of the United States because they are unsatisfied with his policies, that person can and most likely will be arrested, indicted (for a federal offense) and brought to trial for what they may have thought were statements protected by the First Amendment – *"Freedom of Speech."*

As for the Right to *"peaceably"* protest:

Does this mean that a person has the absolute right to protest in public all day and all night without any restriction, despite assembling peacefully? The answer is unequivocally NO!

Public peace overrides our personal right to protest. Therefore, Governors place time restrictions on gatherings involving peaceful protesting.

Amendment II: As established in Amendment II; "The right of the people to keep and bear arms, shall not be infringed."

Does this mean that anyone can possess a firearm freely and walk the streets with a machine gun on their person? The answer is unequivocally NO!

As you may know, in order to "bear arms" in public, a gun permit is required.

Further, in the event a person was to be convicted of a felony offense, there goes their right to "bear arms."

More importantly, if anyone were to "bear arms" after being convicted of a felony offense, they will be prosecuted for being a felon in possession of a firearm, which is a federal offense punishable by a minimum of 5 years in a federal prison.

Are we paying attention?! Where in the United States Constitution does it state that any of the informative examples presented above are illegal and subject to prosecution?

The said illustrations substantiate the very fact that the United States Constitution is vague and can be enigmatic.

What's more, is that Congress at times make matters worse by passing legislation that has repeatedly contradicted the United States Constitution on its face.

Had it not been for the United States Supreme Court Justices who on numberless occasions have ruled Congress' legislative acts to be unconstitutional, we would be residing in a country where the right to privacy would have literally meant that a person must be in their house and by themselves with the doors and blinders closed shut.

To further accentuate on the obscurity of the United States Constitution let's examine the other Five Amendments.

__Amendment IV__: As established in Amendment IV; "The right of the people to be secure in their person, houses, papers and effects, against unreasonable searches and seizures, shall not be violated."

What did the founding fathers mean by "their person?"

Does "their person" denote the clothes that's worn over the naked body?"

And does the term "houses" extend to the garage area and the rest of the property that may be fenced in?

What about "papers" – does this imply all documents that has a person's signature and or handwriting without a person's signature?

And finally, what about "effects" – what does this mean?

Is this not amphibolic and enigmatic? Are the effects limited, restricted and conditional?

Amendment V: As established in Amendment V; "No person shall be held to answer for a capital, or otherwise infamous crime, unless on a presentment or indictment of a grand jury…. Nor shall be compelled in any criminal case to be a witness against himself, nor be deprived of life, liberty or property without due process of law."

The first discernable question is, why didn't the founding fathers start this Amendment with "A person {must} not be held to answer for a capital crime, or otherwise infamous crime, "instead of "No person {shall} be held to answer for a capital or otherwise infamous crime"

When the Bill of Rights was constructed were both terms "shall" and "must" interpreted or understood to have the exact definition?

What is the logical answer to such a complexed and important question?

Further, "capital, or otherwise infamous crime" today translates to mean a felony offense.

Misdemeanors on the other hand are not considered to be "capital, or otherwise infamous crimes."

So, my question to the reader is, did you know, and or would you have understood prior to this explanation that "capital, or otherwise infamous crimes" did not include high-class misdemeanors?

Furthermore, did you know that "presentment or indictment of a grand jury" is required for felony offenses, but not misdemeanor offenses?

Moving along, does "No person shall be held to answer for a capital or otherwise infamous crime, unless on presentment or indictment of a grand jury" denotes that if a person was arrested by a law enforcement officer, and that officer had stated to the person arrested that they were being charged with committing a felony offense, that person "shall" not be detained ("held to answer") without bail absent the "presentment or indictment of a grand jury?"

Or does it denote that a person does not have to go through the fundamental criminal procedures for a felony crime allegedly committed, "unless" they are "indicted by a grand jury?"

Surely the term "held" can be interpreted as "held" imprisoned without bail, or "held"- imprisoned pending the "presentment or indictment of a grand jury."

As for "nor shall be compelled in any criminal case to be a witness against himself."

This is the well-recognized invocation of a person's ***Fifth Amendment Right*** to remain silent and avoid self-incrimination.

But does this mean if granted immunity, that a

judge cannot compel a person to testify, and hold that person in contempt in the event they refuse to testify? The answer is unequivocally NO!

Judges across the United States of America on numerous occasions have held Americans and others in contempt for refusing to testify in court proceedings – an act many Americans would assume to be a violation of their Fifth Amendment Right, but it's not.

And, as for "nor be deprived of life, liberty, or property without due process of law." This implicates three personal factors – (a person's) "life, (a person's) liberty, or (a person's) property," which depending on how "due process is interpreted can consequently present a dangerous result.

Thus, does "deprived of life" mean the government can or cannot execute an American life by lethal injection?

What about deprived of "liberty" – does this mean that a person has the free will to make decisions and choices as they please?

And does a person have the "liberty" (freedom) of not being imprisoned falsely?

What about "due process of law" – is this not troublesome and laborious to comprehend, when there exists the process of

"Federal" and "state" law, which are two independent entities within the same country?

Thus, which "due process of law" is the United States Constitution referring to?

As for deprived of "property" – does this denote a person's house, a person's personal documents, a person's child, and anything that has value, which a person is sole proprietor of?

The gist of all this, is that anyone's "life, liberty or property" can be placed at risk, and put into jeopardy by the government at any moment in their lives, but they would be clueless on how or where to begin defending their fundamental

"*Guaranteed*" Constitutional Rights, due to the lack of education on the United States constitution.

These are the consequences of depriving oneself from the education that's necessary, compulsory and imperative.

Although, the language found inside the Bill of Rights is ambiguous, indecisive and perplexing, the United States Supreme Court Justices have provided precise and detailed explanations, which we can read, study and become familiar with.

<u>Amendment VI</u>: As established in Amendment VI:

"In all criminal prosecutions, the accused shall enjoy the right to a speedy and public trial, by an impartial jury of the states and district wherein the crime shall have been committed …. be confronted with witness against him, to have compulsory process for obtaining witnesses in his favor; and to have assistance of counsel for his defense."

The said Amendment specifically deals with the substantial issues surrounding our criminal justice systematic procedures.

In all criminal prosecutions, Amendment VI of the United States Constitution covers "the right to a speedy trail and public trial"; the right to "an impartial jury;" the right to "be confronted with witnesses in (a person's) favor;" and the right "to have assistance of counsel for (a person's) defense."

Here, we will find illustrations that will demonstrate the difficulties of trying to understand the United States Constitution absent any real investigation challenge.

For instance, at first glance "the right to a speedy trial and public trial" may appear to be easily understood.

However, a second look with a magnifying eye, would raise a pattern of questions.

Like, what time frame must elapse in order to invoke the speedy trial right?

Is it days, months, or years, and does this apply to every state and municipal court in United States of America?

Also, does "public trial" denote that the entire public can sit in, observe the trial, and video record the entire trial?

I find it baffling and nonsensical how most if not all state courts allow video recording throughout the entire trial in celebrity cases, or in a case implicating significant consequences, so that the public could witness the proceedings, but video recording in a trial within any federal court proceeding, regardless of the status of the defendant is prohibited.

"An impartial jury" also seems to be clear in language, but what if a person is black or Latin American, and that person has an all-white jury in a state that's predominately white people or vice-versa, would this be considered an impartial jury?

What about the right to "be confronted with witnesses against" the person who is in trial?

Does this mean that a dead person's statement cannot be introduced as evidence in a trial?

And, what about the right "to have compulsory process for obtaining witnesses in (a person's) favor?

Does this mean that if a defendant's attorney had

failed to call witnesses that may have been in the defendant's favor, but may not have changed the results of a guilty verdict, that the defendants sixth Amendment Right was violated?

Further, what does the right "to have the assistance of counsel for (a person's) defense" mean?

Does it mean that the court must provide a defendant with "the assistance of counsel" regardless if the defendant has finances enabling them to hire and pay for their own attorney?

And finally, does "for his defense" mean, that an attorney must or "shall" articulate a defense strategy consistent with the defendant's theory of defense, or is an attorney at liberty to present a defense that they feel due to their experience is the best approach, despite the defendant being in total disagreement?

Be mindful, although I use the term "defendant" in the above illustrations, the question presented and their respective answers (which for some, I purposely did not provide an answer for) can affect anyone – including YOU!!

Amendment VIII: As established in Amendment VIII; "Excessive bail shall not be required."

Does mean, that a person arrested and charged with a

misdemeanor "shall" be released on their own recognizance?

And does it mean in the case of a "serial killer" and or a "rapist," that "excessive bail (or held without bail to protect society) shall not be required?

As for "no cruel and unusual punishments inflicted;" does this mean that life sentences and 10 years or more imposed sentences by Judges for non-violent offenses should be considered "cruel and unusual punishments inflicted?"

And does this mean, that the institutions where prisoners are being held in shall not inflict "cruel and unusual punishments?"

What did the founding fathers really intend when they structured the Eight Amendment?"

Amendment XIV: As established in Amendment XIV (Section 1); "No state shall make or enforce any law which shall abridge the privileges or immunities of citizens of the United States; nor shall any state deprive any person of life, liberty, or property, without due process of law; nor deny to any person with its jurisdiction the equal protection of the laws."

What does shall not "abridge the privileges or immunities of citizens of the United States" mean?

More importantly, what "privileges or immunities"

does a United States citizen possess?

The only way to learn about the "privileges or immunities" that are safeguarded by Amendment XIV is by way of educating yourself.

Is it not of major importance to be informed of the "privileges or immunities" that YOU as an American citizen are entitled to?

As for, "nor shall any state deprive any person life, liberty, or property, without due process of law;" this part of Amendment XIV is identical to the language used in Amendment V with the exception of the words "any state."

Here, a shadow of clarity is provided by using the

words "any state."

However, the end part of the sentence, without due process of law" is still up in the air.

In other words, which "due process of law" were the founding fathers alluding to?

Were they alluding to Federal Law or State Law?

And what did they mean by "nor deny to any person within its jurisdiction the equal protection of the laws?"

In this section of Amendment XIV, the term "law" is pluralized – "laws."

Thus, does "equal protection of the laws" denote that whatever jurisdiction a person may be in, the law of the State where they are residents of must apply?

And if not applied, would this essentially be considered a denial of "equal protection of the {laws}?"

In concluding this treatise, and with respect to the ambiguities that exist within the Bill of Rights, (United States Constitution) and the inescapable problems dealing with "RACISM" and "POLITICS" in our country, I must inform the readers that I designedly abstained from supplying what would have required extensive detailed answers.

My main objective was to provide a brief influence of

acquired facts entailing matters of contention that are paramount and salient, especially in areas that involve our safety, protection and Constitutional Rights.

More importantly, I pray this treatise incites an enthusiastic desire to jaunt on an educational voyage around the world of beneficial knowledge.

Certainly, and I say this with sincerity, the substantive leading issues presented herein are severe and relevant to our independency, autonomy, emancipation and sovereignty.

I respectfully extend an invitation to the intellectual minds, commentators, legal scholars and authors of pure educational knowledge to the perquisite of explicating in detail the abstruse subjects I've promulgated in this treatise.

Finally, the word "treatise" is usually used by Politicians – Senators, House of Representatives etc. and is spoken as to a call to arms.

So even though we are not fighting a conventional enemy on a conventional battlefield, make no mistake, we are with an ephemeral enemy who threatens the fundamental development of the youth of our great country, by denying them a full and proper education.

I hope this treatise was enjoyed. It was my pleasure presenting a brief but hopefully impactful reminder

of the importance in seeking
an education on all levels.

141

"EDUCATION IS THE KEY"

FINAL WORD

EDUCATION – IS – EXTRAORDINARY – EDUCATION – IS – ETERNITY

EDUCATION – IS – EXCELLENCE – EDUCATION – IS – ECONOMICS

EDUCATION – IS – EXCITEMENT – EDUCATION – IS – EDIFICATION

EDUCATION – IS – EQUALITY – EDUCATION – IS – ELEMENTARY

EDUCATION – IS – EVOLUTION – EDUCATION – IS – ENERGY

*EDUCATION – IS –
ENDOWMENT – EDUCATION
– IS ESSENTIAL*

Embrace Education and
Education will Provide YOU
with the Meaning of Life YOU
so desire!!

www.ingramcontent.com/pod-product-compliance
Lightning Source LLC
Chambersburg PA
CBHW071626150726
48000CB00004B/1903